Saving
Wild Wolves

Written by Anna Porter

Flying Start
to Literacy®

Contents

Introduction

Wolves used to live in many places around the world. They lived as wild animals and killed other wild animals for food.

But as farmers and their animals moved into the places where wolves lived, wolves were seen as a problem and many were killed. Because of this, wolves became endangered and threatened with extinction.

wild wolf cubs

Now some people want to protect wolves. They capture wolves and take them to wolf refuge centres to protect them so they can breed. The wolf cubs are looked after at the centre until they are at least one year old. When the wolves are strong enough to look after themselves, they are released back into the wild. This will help to build up the number of wolves in the wild.

But protecting wolves makes some farmers and hunters very unhappy. They still believe wolves should be killed.

This red wolf has just been released back into the wild.

Chapter 1:
Wolves in the wild

Wolves are wild animals that live in the forests and the mountains in North America, Europe and Asia. They come from the same animal family as dogs, but they are much bigger and stronger than most dogs.

Wolves eat other animals. They are carnivores. Wolves hunt at night and feed mainly on prey such as deer, caribou, elk and moose. They also eat smaller animals such as beavers, rats and hares. Wolves are wary of people and run away when they see them.

Wild wolf fact

Wolves are the largest members of the dog family.

When a wolf is alone in the wild, it howls to communicate with other wolves in its pack.

Wolves live and hunt together in groups called packs. Each wolf in a pack has a role. The leader of the pack is the dominant or strongest wolf. This means that the other wolves in the pack have to show it respect.

Each wolf pack stays in an area of land where they hunt and raise their young. This area is known as the wolves' territory.

a pack of wolves

Wolves mark their territory by leaving their scent all over it. Wolves defend their territory from other wolves by fighting them or killing them.

Wolf howls

Wolves howl in different ways to greet other wolves in their pack, or to tell these wolves where they are and mark out their territory. They hold their head and mouth in different positions and snarl at each other to argue or fight.

This snarl means that this wolf is the dominant one.

This snarl means the wolf may be trying to be the new dominant wolf.

Chapter 2:
Wolves and people

Long ago, there were groups of people who lived close to where wolves lived. These people did not fear wolves.

Many Native Americans respected wolves. They watched how the wolves hunted in packs and modelled their own hunting skills on what the wolves did.

Many groups of Native Americans used the image of the wolf to decorate totem poles and other ceremonial objects.

They also admired the way wolves worked together to protect and care for the members of their pack, and they liked how the wolves defended their territory.

The Pawnee

The Native American Pawnee tribe were known as the Wolf People. They carved and painted pictures of wolves on rocks and cliffs throughout parts of North America. They rubbed wolf fur on their arrows and carried small things in pouches made from wolf skin. They believed that by doing this, the spirit of the wolf would be passed on to them and help them to be better at hunting for food.

The Pawnee painted their faces white to look like wolves. They wore wolf skins over their bodies and heads, and walked on their arms and legs to look like wolves. They believed that doing this would make them strong and clever like wolves and help them travel long distances to look for food.

When new settlers arrived in North America, they painted pictures of how the Native Americans hunted buffalo on the plains. This picture shows the hunters disguised in wolf skins.

New settlers

When new groups of people moved to North America to live, some settled in places where wolves lived. They cut down trees and cleared the land so they could build farms, ranches, houses and roads.

The farmers brought cattle and sheep to these places and planted new grasses and crops for their animals. This changed the land in the places where wolves lived. The wild animals that the wolves hunted moved away.

The wolves needed to find new animals to eat in the places that they had marked out as their own territory, so they ate the farm animals.

New settlers built their farms and houses in the places where wild wolves lived.

15

Chapter 3:

Why were so many wolves killed?

The new settlers were scared of wolves, and both farmers and hunters killed them.

Farmers

Farmers did not like wolves because wolves killed their farm animals. Wolves hunted in packs and killed a large number of farm animals each night.

To protect their farm animals, the farmers killed the wolves. They trapped, shot or poisoned any wolves they could find. The farmers argued that they needed their farm animals to make a living, and if wolves killed their animals, the farmers lost a lot of money.

The wolves hunted farm animals such as cattle and sheep when they were hungry.

Hunters

Many hunters did not like wolves because the wolves killed their hunting dogs. They had trained their dogs to help them find animals to hunt. So the hunters killed the wolves and used their fur for clothing and rugs.

Wolves and dogs are from the same animal family, and the wolves saw the dogs invading their territory. This made the wolves want to defend their territory, so they killed the hunting dogs.

Hunters liked to go into
forests to shoot wild ducks,
deer, elk, bears and
other animals.

Chapter 4:
Protecting wolves

As time passed, more and more wolves were killed and their numbers in the wild became very low. People who wanted to protect the wolves believed that farmers should not set up their farms in the places where wolves lived. They also argued that hunters should not take dogs into forests where wolves lived.

For many years, nothing was done. The number of wolves living in the wild decreased.

Saving red wolves

By 1980, only 14 red wolves were left in North America. These wolves were captured and taken to a wolf refuge centre to protect them. A breeding program was set up to increase their numbers and save them from becoming extinct. People also bred and raised red wolves in zoos.

These actions have helped red wolf numbers to grow again. Some of these red wolves have been put back in wild areas that have been set aside for them. The wolves have now bred in their own territory, and about 100 red wolves survive in the wild today.

Wild wolf fact

In 1980, the red wolf was listed as extinct in the wild. This meant that there were no red wolves living in the wild. The only red wolves in the world were the 14 in captivity.

These red wolf cubs
were born at a
wolf refuge centre.

Saving grey wolves

In 1973, the grey wolf was listed as endangered. It was thought that numbers were so low that it could become extinct in the wild. Many of the places where these wolves lived had been taken over by farms and houses. The areas where the wolves lived became smaller and smaller.

People who wanted to protect the grey wolves set aside land for the wolves to live naturally, away from houses, farms or ranches.

Grey wolves have now been put back into wildlife parks in North America. A large area of land that runs between several of these wildlife parks is being set aside for the wolves so they can live in their packs and eat wild animals.

Conclusion

There will always be arguments between different groups of people about whether or not wolves should be protected.

The number of wild wolves has now increased in some states in the USA. But the number of farms and houses near the wolves' territories keeps increasing too. This means some people are still losing their farm animals and pets. They think that wolves are a big problem and want them killed. But others are working very hard to protect them and help them to breed.

Index

A note from the author

I grew up on a farm that was surrounded by forests where many wild animals lived. I often went for long walks to observe these animals in the wild. When I travelled to North America to visit national parks, I was lucky to observe wolves in the wild and at wolf refuges where people looked after wolves. But I also met farmers who thought they should be destroyed.

This made me think about the discussions I had with people who thought some wild animals were pests and should be destroyed, so I decided to write a book about this issue.